Voyages in English
Writing and Grammar

Carolyn Marie Dimick
General Editor

Marie T. McVey
Revision Editor

Jeanne M. Baker
Carolyn Marie Dimick
Susan Mary Platt
Joan I. Rychalsky
Authors

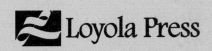 Loyola Press

Contributors
Beth Duncan
Diane Gonciarz
Jan Marcus
Cathy Ann Tell
Richard Weisenseel

Editors
Margaret O'Leary Coyle
Catherine Marcic Joyce

Production
Mary Bowers
Genevieve Kelley
Ellie Knepler
Anne Marie Mastandrea
Carla Jean Mayer
Julia Mayer
Molly O'Halloran
Jill Smith
Leslie Uriss

Cover Design
Steve Straus, Think Design

Cover Art
Jessie Coates,
Old Port Hudson

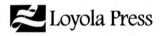

Loyola Press

3441 North Ashland Avenue
Chicago, Illinois 60657
1-800-621-1008

ISBN 0-8294-0981-5

Printed in the United States of America

00 01 02   5 4 3

Table of Contents

CHAPTER 1

Readiness

Table of Contents

CHAPTER 2

Class Story

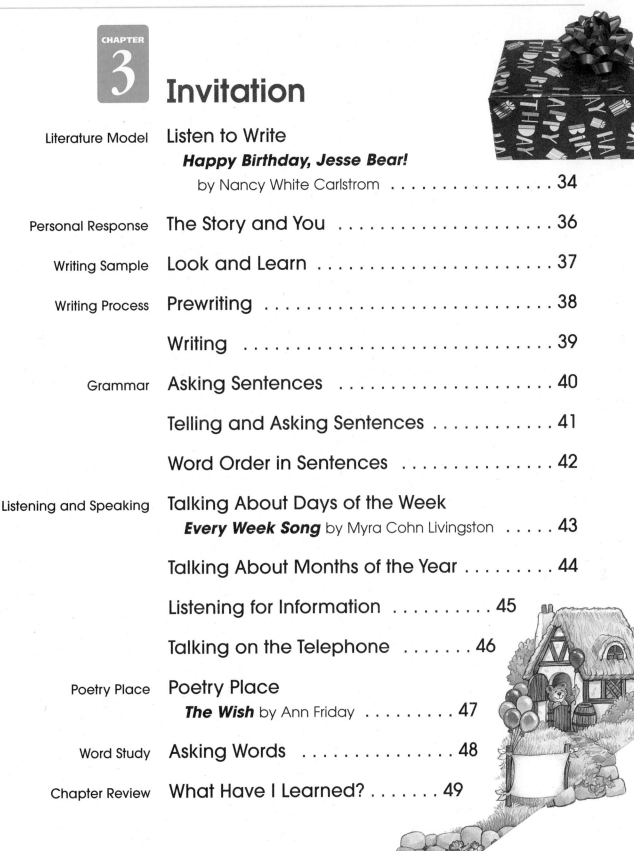

v

Table of Contents

Personal Narrative

Table of Contents

Personal Note

Table of Contents

Friendly Letter

CHAPTER 9

Report

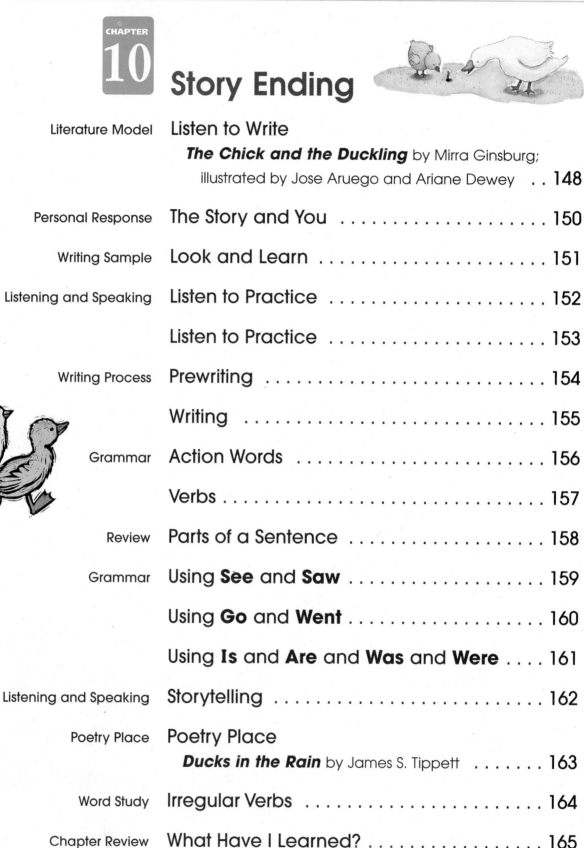

Story Ending

CHAPTER 1

Readiness

Colors

Draw and color to complete the picture.

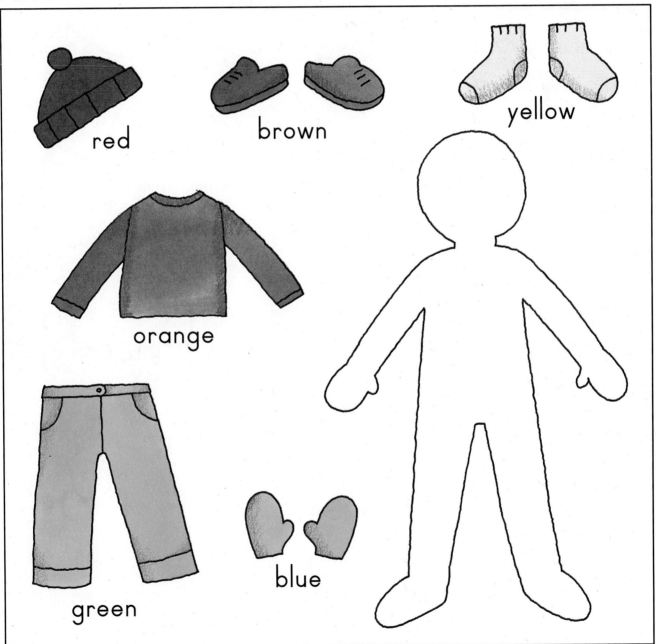

red

brown

yellow

orange

green

blue

Read the color words.

Color the picture.

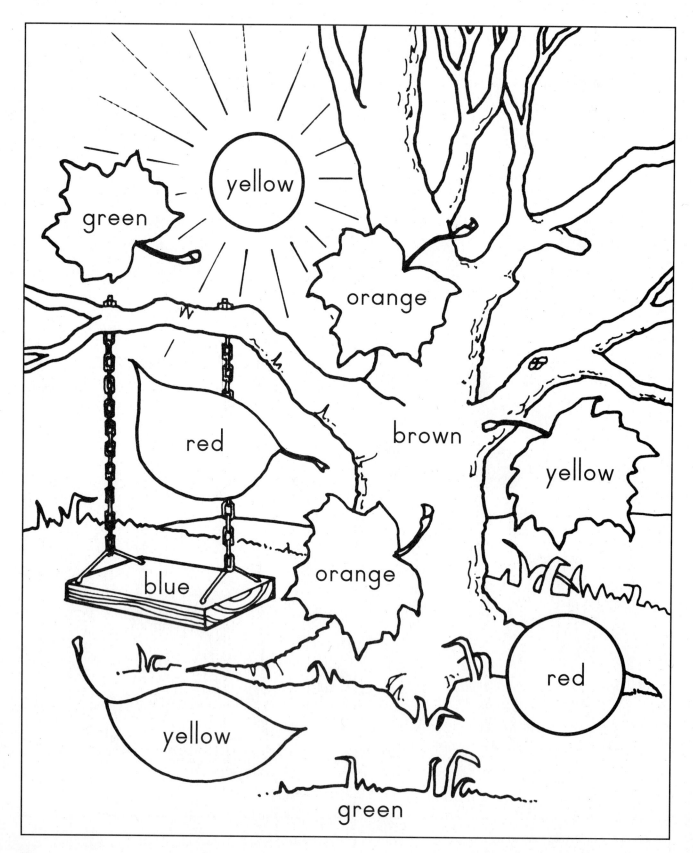

Top, Middle, Bottom

Draw a flower in the top box.
Draw a ball in the middle box.
Draw a bug in the bottom box.

top

middle

bottom

In, On, Over, Under

Listen.

Then color the picture.

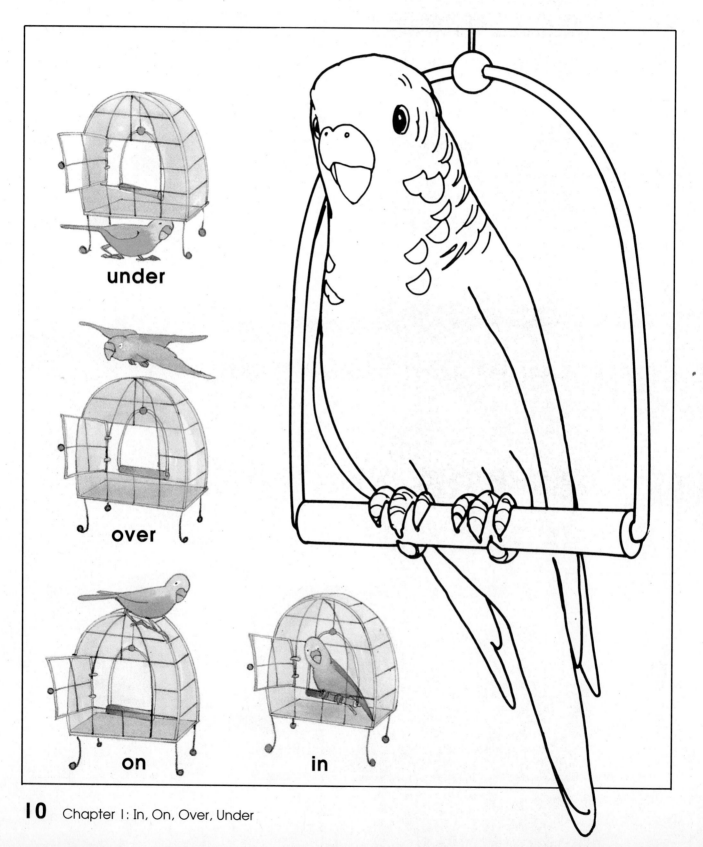

under

over

on

in

Big and Little

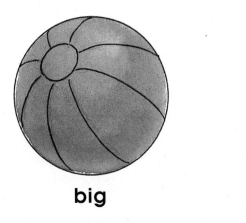

big   little

 Color the box under each big thing blue.

 Color the box under each little thing red.

Left and Right

Listen.

Then draw.

left   right

Picture Order

Listen to the rhymes.

Number the pictures in order.

The Alphabet

Trace the letters.

Trace the letters.

Time to Rhyme

Listen to the poem.
Draw a picture to finish each rhyme.

Little Chickens

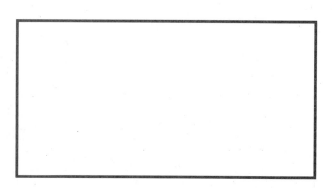

Said the first little chicken
With an odd little squirm,
"I wish I would find
a fat little ___."

Said the second little chicken
With an odd little shrug,
"I wish I would find
a fat little ___."

Said the third little chicken
With an odd little sigh,
"I wish I would find
a fat little ___."

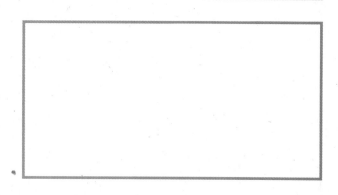

Name _____

Parts of a Story

Listen to a story.
Look at the pictures.

beginning

middle

end

Class Story

Listen to Write

Albert's Field Trip

by Leslie Tryon

I.

2.

3.

The Story and You

Which part of **Albert's Field Trip** did you like best?

Circle that picture.

Write about why you liked it.

Name _____

Look and Learn

Read what the class wrote about the trip.
Everyone helped write the story.

Our Class Trip

We went to an apple farm.
There were so many trees.
We picked lots of apples.
We had juice and pie.
It was fun.

Prewriting

Your class is going to the zoo.
What might you see there?
Draw some things you may see.

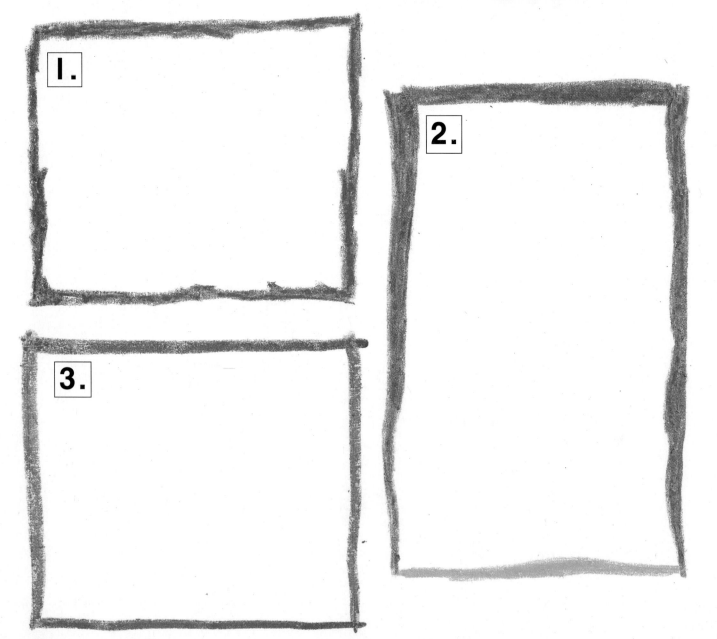

1.

2.

3.

Name _____

Writing

Choose one of your pictures on page 22. Draw it in the box.
Then write about your picture.

_____
_____
_____
_____

Sentences

A **sentence** is a group of words that tells a whole idea.

This is a sentence:
    The children pick apples.
This is not a sentence:
    the children

Draw a line under each sentence.

1. The class goes on a trip.

2. a big bus

3. The trees are full of apples.

4. big and little apples

5. The apples are good.

Telling Sentences

A **telling sentence** tells a whole idea.
A **telling sentence** begins with a capital letter.
A **telling sentence** ends with a ⬚.

This is a telling sentence:
The driver stops the bus.

Read each telling sentence.
Trace the capital letter at the beginning.
Make a ⬚ at the end.

1. __W__e all sing on the bus ⬚

2. __T__he bus goes over hills ⬚

3. __T__here is a big red barn ⬚

4. __A__ll of us go inside ⬚

Word Order in Sentences

Words in a sentence are in an order that makes sense.

These words are in order:
 The apple farm is big.
These words are not in order:
 big The is apple farm

Are the words in the right order?
Draw a line under each sentence.

1. Some apples are green.

2. picked many apples We

3. I take an apple to the driver.

4. We all eat apples.

Name _____

Listening to and Singing a Song

Here are the words to a song you may know.
Listen and sing.

 **The Wheels on the Bus**
traditional song (adaptation)

The wheels on the bus go 'round and 'round,
'round and 'round, 'round and 'round.
The wheels on the bus go 'round and 'round,
all around the town.

The driver of our bus says, "Sing a song!
Sing a song! Sing a song!"
The driver on our bus says, "Sing a song!"
all around the town.

The kids on the bus sing, "We're going to the farm!
We're going to the farm! We're going to the farm!"
The kids on the bus sing, "We're going to the farm!"
all around the town.

Expressing an Opinion

Look at each picture.
Does it show a good place for a class trip?
Circle a face to show how you would feel.

1.

2.

3.

Name _____

Sharing Experiences

Let's talk about places you've visited.
Read the list.
Make an X to mark things you have done.

☐ **1.** I've been to the zoo.

☐ **2.** I've been to the ocean.

☐ **3.** I've been to the museum.

Draw a picture to show one place you have visited.

Listening for Details

Listen.

Circle the picture that shows the answer about the trip.

1. What did everyone see first?

2. What did everyone get?

3. What did everyone eat?

4. What will the children plant at school?

Poetry Place

One, Two, Three, Four

One, two, three, four,
Mary at the cottage door,
Five, six, seven, eight,
Eating apples off a plate.

Words with Similar Meanings

Some words mean almost the same thing.

The words **big** and **large** mean almost the same thing.
The bus is big.
The bus is large.

Draw a line to match words
that mean almost the same thing.

1. glad • • small

2. lots • • happy

3. little • • many

4. tired • • turn

5. spin • • sleepy

What Have I Learned?

Does each group of words form a sentence?
Make a ⬚ **at the end if the words form a sentence.**

1. The trip is over ⬚

2. It is late ⬚

3. all the children ⬚

4. They go home ⬚

5. so sleepy ⬚

Invitation

Listen to Write

Happy Birthday, Jesse Bear!

by Nancy White Carlstrom

1.

2.

3.

4.

5.

6.

The Story and You

What birthday gift would you take
to Jesse Bear?
Draw a picture.
Write about the picture.

Look and Learn

Jesse Bear wants you to come to his party, too.
Read his invitation.

To: _____

What: A birthday party

Where: My house

When: Friday at 4:00

From: Jesse Bear

Prewriting

Look at the pictures.

Circle where the party will be.

Circle when the party will be.

Name _____

Writing

Who will come to your party?
Write the person's name.
Now look back at page 38.
Finish writing the invitation.

To: _____

What: _____

Where: _____

When: _____

Asking Sentences

An **asking sentence** asks a question.

An **asking sentence** begins with a capital letter.

An **asking sentence** ends with a ?

This is an asking sentence.

How old are you?

Read each asking sentence.

Trace the capital letter.

Make a ? at the end.

1. __W__here is the sign ☐

2. __C__an we come in ☐

3. __W__hen will we play ☐

4. __I__s the cake ready ☐

Party!

Telling and Asking Sentences

Make a **.** at the end of each telling sentence.

Make a **?** at the end of each asking sentence.

1. Here are the candles
2. Who will light them
3. Jesse makes a wish
4. Will you share some cake
5. The party is fun

Word Order in Sentences

The words in a sentence must be in an order that makes sense.

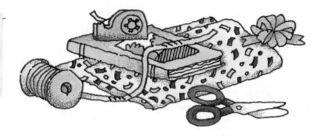

Trace to show how to put these words in order.

the book Jesse Bear reads.

Jesse Bear reads

the book.

Write to show how to put these words in order.

1. is big The book.

_____

_____

2. the pictures He likes.

_____

_____

3. good The story is.

_____

_____

_____

Talking About Days of the Week

Listen.

Talk about what you do on the days of the week.

Sunday Monday Tuesday Wednesday

Thursday Friday Saturday

Thursday Friday Saturday

Every Week Song

by Myra Cohn Livingston

What is the day after Sunday?
  Monday.
Tuesday and Wednesday and then
  Thursday and
  Friday and
  Saturday
And then we begin again . . .

Wednesday Tuesday Monday Sunday

Talking About Months of the Year

Listen and then repeat the names of the months.

January
February
March
April
May
June
July
August
September
October
November
December

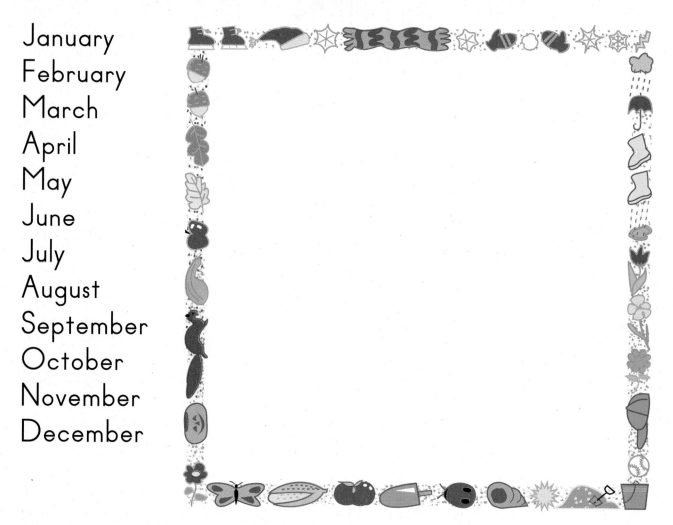

Draw a picture of you on your birthday.

When is your birthday?

Write the month.

Write the number of the day.

_____   _____

- - - - - - - - - - - - - -   - - - - - - - - - - - -

_____   _____

Name

Listening for Information

1. Who?

2. Where?

3. When?

4. What?

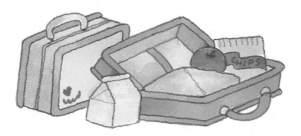

Talking on the Telephone

What do you do when you call someone?
What do you do when someone calls you?
Put an X in the box next to what you do.

To make a call
- ☐ I press the numbers carefully.
- ☐ I speak clearly.
- ☐ I tell my name.
- ☐ I say what I want.
- ☐ I listen.
- ☐ I say thank you.

To answer a call
- ☐ I speak clearly.
- ☐ I find out who is calling.
- ☐ I ask someone to come to the phone or
- ☐ I take a message.
- ☐ I say thank you.

Poetry Place

The Wish

by Ann Friday

Each birthday wish
I've ever made
Really does come true.
Each year I wish
I'll grow some more
And every year
    I
        DO!

Asking Words

Asking words begin sentences that ask questions.

Here are some asking words:

Who

What

Where

When

Why

Write an asking word to finish each question.

1. _____ is in the box?

2. _____ is it from?

3. _____ is the birthday boy?

4. _____ will he open the box?

5. _____ is he smiling?

Name _____

What Have I Learned?

Write **A** before each asking sentence.
Write **T** before each telling sentence.
Draw a line under each asking word.

1. _____ The party is over.

2. _____ Who will clean up?

3. _____ Papa puts things away.

4. _____ Why does the little bear help?

5. _____ Where is the little bear?

CHAPTER 4

Personal Narrative

Listen to Write

My Brown Bear Barney

by Dorothy Butler

illustrated by Elizabeth Fuller

1.

2.

3.

4.

5.

6.

7.

8.

The Story and You

Think about the places the girl takes Barney.
Pick the place you like best.
Draw and write about you and Barney
having fun there.

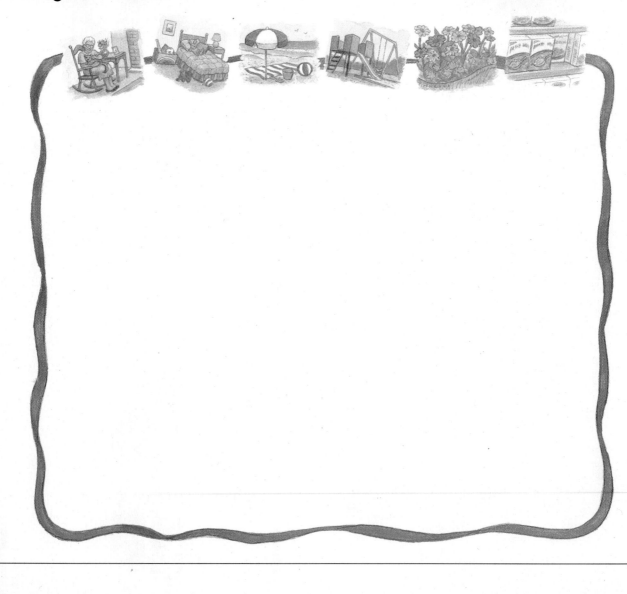

_____

- - - - - - - - - - - - - - - - - - - -

_____

_____

- - - - - - - - - - - - - - - - - - - -

_____

Name _____

Look and Learn

Look at the picture.
Read what Josh writes
about himself.

My name is Josh.
I have lots of toys.
I like my toy dog
Spot the best.

Recall Details

Listen.

Circle the pictures of things the girl takes with her.

Listen.

Draw one thing the girl takes to the beach.

Compare and Contrast

Look.

How are Barney and Spot the same?

How are they different?

	Barney	Spot
toy	✔	✔
brown		
spotted		
4 legs		
tail		

Prewriting

Tell about yourself.

Look at the words and pictures in each box.

Put an X next to each thing you like.

1.

__ my toys   __ my books   __ my friends

2.

__ to ride   __ to draw   __ to read

3.

__ the park   __ the beach   __ the zoo

Name _____

Writing

Write to tell about yourself.
Use words you marked on page 56
to finish each sentence.

1. I like _____ .

2. I like _____ .

3. I like to go to _____ .

Draw a picture to go with your sentences.

Naming Words

Words that name people, places, or things are called **naming words**.

People	Places	Things
sister	zoo	apple
man	park	book
teacher	school	cup

Circle the naming words.

1. The girl swims at the beach.

2. The boy flies a kite.

3. The moon is in the sky.

4. I ride the bus to school.

Name _____

Words That Name One and More Than One

Add -s to make a naming word mean more than one.

bear   bears

Look at each picture. Read the naming word.
Write the naming word with -s if the picture
shows more than one.

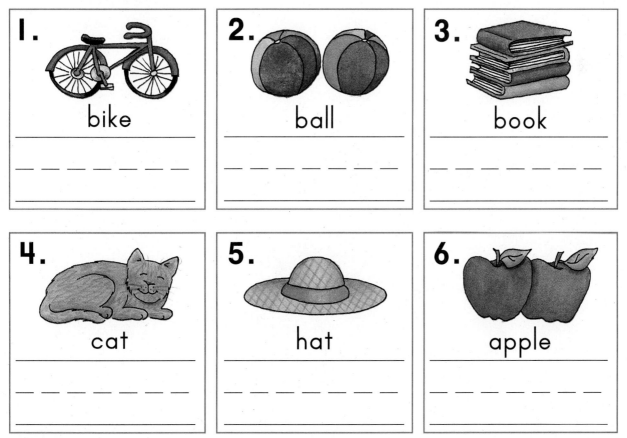

1. bike
_____

2. ball
_____

3. book
_____

4. cat
_____

5. hat
_____

6. apple
_____

Asking Sentences

An **asking sentence** asks a question.
It often begins with an asking word.

Trace the first letter of each asking word.
Make a [?] at the end of the sentence.

1. __W__hen will we go out ☐

2. __W__here is my toy ☐

3. __W__ho will we see ☐

4. __W__hat game can we play ☐

Name _____

Talking About Special Names

Look at the picture.
Read the sentences.

The boy is in the park with the dog.
Josh is in the park with Spot.

The words Josh and Spot are special naming words.

Use special naming words to tell about each picture.

1.

2.

3.

Using I, Me, and My

You can use the words **I**, me, and **my** to tell about yourself.

This is my bear. I take him with me.

Draw yourself in the picture.
Then use the words **I**, me, and **my** to tell about the picture.

Responding to Asking Sentences

Read what the asking sentence asks.

Look at the picture.

Say a telling sentence to give the answer.

1. Who reads?

2. Do the bears have hats?

3. Where is the dog?

4. Are the apples red?

Listening for Rhymes

Say each picture name.

Listen to the sentences.

Write the picture name that makes a rhyme.

1. A <u>cat</u> puts on a __.   hat   wig

Oh! A cat is in a _____!

2. A <u>bug</u> sits on a __.   box   rug

Oh! A bug is on a _____!

3. A <u>frog</u> hops on a __.   log   chair

Oh! A frog is on a _____!

Name

My Teddy Bear

by Marchette Chute

A teddy bear is a faithful friend.
You can pick him up at either end.
His fur is the color of breakfast toast,
And he's always there when you need him most.

Compound Words

Some words are really two smaller words put together.

mail + box = mailbox
cup + cake = cupcake

Look at the cupcake. I made it myself!

Read the first sentence.
Put together the words with lines under them.
Write the new word.

1. My doll lives in this house.

It is a _____.

2. I sail my boat.

It is a _____.

3. Mili and Téa jump over the rope.

It is a _____.

4. I paint with a thin brush.

It is a _____.

Name _____

What Have I Learned?

Naming words can name **one** person, place, or thing or **more than one** person, place, and thing.

Look at the things in the picture.
Read the naming words.
Write each naming word in a box.

birds

shell

pail

chairs

One	More Than One

© Loyola Press

Listen to Write

Too Many Tamales

by Gary Soto

illustrated by Ed Martinez

1.

2.

3.

4.

5.

6.

The Story and You

Maria liked pretty things.

She cut out pictures of things she liked.

Draw some things you like.

Tell about your pictures.

_____

_ _

_____

_____

_____

Look and Learn

Maria tells how to make tamales.

1. I get _____ .

2. I knead _____ .

3. I spread _____ .

4. I add _____ .

5. Mom folds _____ .

6. Dad boils _____ .

7. I EAT!

Prewriting

Write words to tell what to do.

Use the words and pictures from the box.

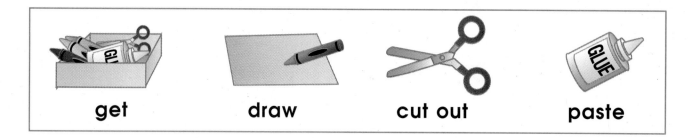

get draw cut out paste

How to Make a Mask

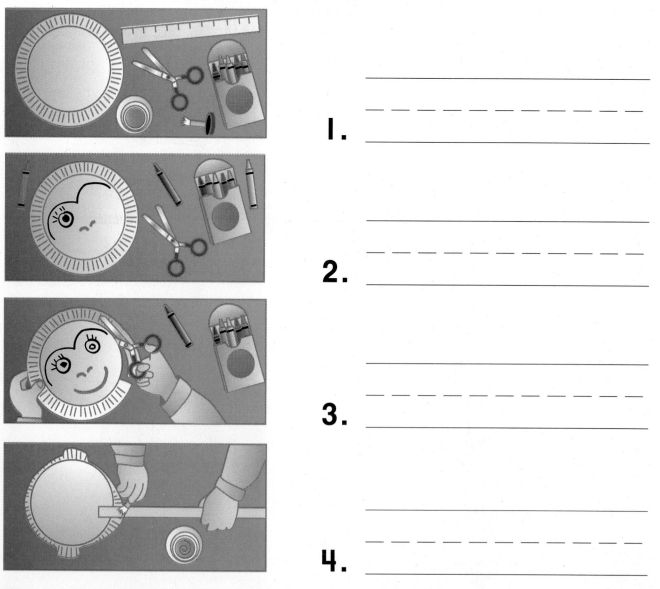

1. _____

2. _____

3. _____

4. _____

Name _____

Writing

Write to tell how to make a mask.
Use your list on page 72.

How to Make a Mask

_____

1. I get _____ .

_____

2. I _____ .

_____

3. I _____ .

_____

4. I _____ .

a bear   **a rabbit**   **a frog**

Action Words

An **action word** tells what a person, animal, or thing does.

The action word in the sentence is **eat.**
It tells what the friends do.

The friends eat.

Circle the action words. Write them.

1. The girls play. _____

2. The dog barks. _____

3. The frog hops. _____

4. The cats sleep. _____

Name _____

Action Words with One

An **action word** that tells what **one** person, animal, or thing does ends with -**s**.

Trace the action word.
Write -s at the end to make the action word correct in the sentence.

1. The bear dance ____ .

2. The frog sing ____ .

3. The cow play ____ a horn.

4. Maria clap ____ .

Action Words with More Than One

An **action word** that tells about more than one person, animal, or thing does not end in **-s**.

Write the correct action word in each sentence.

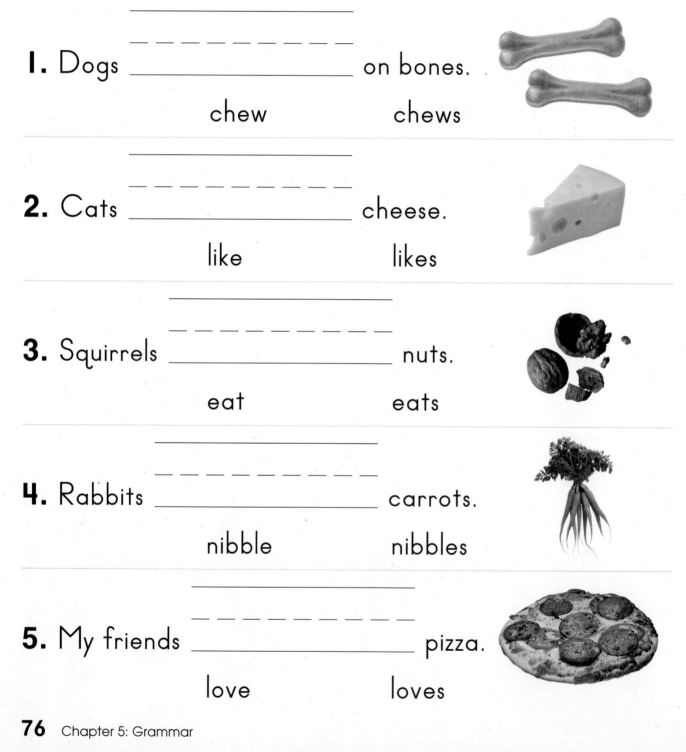

1. Dogs _____ on bones.

            chew   chews

2. Cats _____ cheese.

            like   likes

3. Squirrels _____ nuts.

            eat   eats

4. Rabbits _____ carrots.

            nibble   nibbles

5. My friends _____ pizza.

            love   loves

Name _____

Naming Words

Write the correct naming word in each sentence.

1. The _____ cooks.

boy   boys

2. His _____ nap.

pal   pals

3. The _____ smells the food.

bear   bears

4. The _____ eat.

friend   friends

Using Action Words

Listen to this action-word song.
Add new action words to the song.
Sing and act out the words.

jump	wave	stir
creep	tap	run

Clap Your Hands

by Charles Seeger

Clap, clap, clap your hands,
Clap your hands together.
Clap, clap, clap your hands,
Clap your hands together.

Shake, shake, shake the beat,
Shake the beat together.
Shake, shake, shake the beat,
Shake the beat together.

Name _____

Riddles with Action Words

Listen to the riddles.

Draw a line from the riddle to the picture

that shows the answer.

1. I wiggle my long ears.
I hop all around.
What am I?   •   •

2. I run on four legs.
I growl so loud.
What am I?   •   •

3. I eat flies.
I say "ribbet, ribbet."
What am I?   •   •

Make up your own riddle about an animal.

Put two action words in your riddle.

Working in a Small Group

Maria asked her cousins for help.
Working together can make a big job easier.

Talk about these rules for working with others.

1. Share ideas.
Talk about what you need to do.

2. Listen to each other.
Everyone has ideas to share.

3. Share jobs.
Everyone can help.

4. Plan your work.
Talk about how long it will take
each one to do a part.

Name _____

Poetry Place

Mix a Pancake

by Christina Rossetti

Mix a pancake,
Stir a pancake
Pop it in the pan;
Fry the pancake,
Toss the pancake—
Catch it if you can.

First, Next, Last

**Write the words first, next, and last
to show the order.**

1.

_____   _____   _____

— — — — — — —   — — — — — — —   — — — — — — —

_____   _____   _____

2.

_____   _____   _____

— — — — — — —   — — — — — — —   — — — — — — —

_____   _____   _____

Name _____

What Have I Learned?

Remember, if the sentence tells what only one person, animal, or thing does, use an action word with **-s** at the end.

Write an action word from the box to finish each sentence.

| slides | swings | hops | climbs |
| slide | swing | hop | climb |

1. The bears _____.

2. The frog _____.

3. The rabbit _____.

4. The dogs _____.

Listen to Write

I Speak, I Say, I Talk

by Arnold L. Shapiro

The Story and You

Circle the picture of one animal.
Write the sound the animal makes.

Name _____

Look and Learn

Here is a new poem.
It tells about animal sounds, too.

Cats meow.
Chicks peep.
Hippos grunt.
But I speak!
I say!
I talk!

Prewriting

Pick three animals to write a poem about.

Write the names of the animals.
Write words that tell the sounds they make.

Names

Sounds

1. _____

_____

2. _____

_____

3. _____

tigers

pigs

dogs

snakes

turkeys

bears

Name _____

Writing

Write your poem.

Use what you wrote in the chart on page 88.

But I speak !

I say !

I talk !

Draw little pictures around your poem.

Action Words with More Than One

Action words that tell what more than one person or thing does do not end with -s.

The sentence tells about more than one duck. No -s is at the end of the word **quack**.

The ducks quack.

Write -s at the end of the action word if it is needed.

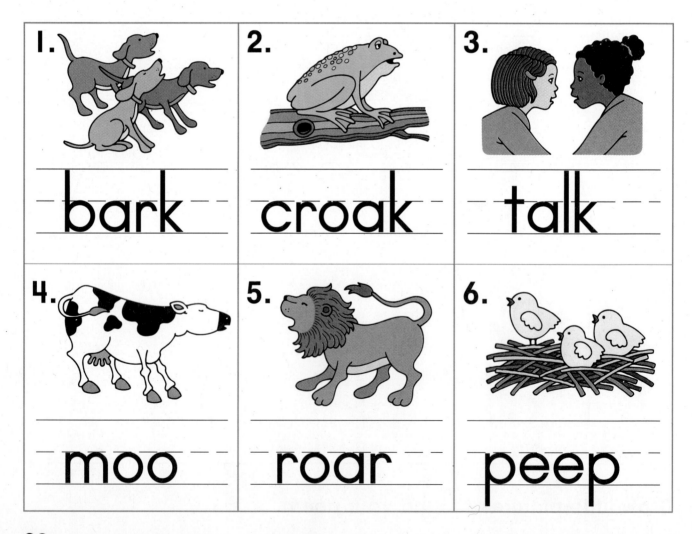

1. bark

2. croak

3. talk

4. moo

5. roar

6. peep

Name _____

More Action Words

Write the correct action word.

1. The bears _____.

      run   runs

2. The pigs _____.

      yell   yells

3. A frog _____.

      wave   waves

4. Some birds _____.

      clap   claps

Action Words with One

Write an action word to finish each sentence about the picture.

tap	toot	sing	beat
taps	toots	sings	beats

1. The girl _____ .

2. A duck _____ the drum.

3. The cat _____ her foot.

4. A bear _____ the horn.

Name _____

Listen to Chime In

Look and listen.
When you are ready, say the words, too.

You Can't Make a Turtle Come Out

by Malvina Reynolds

You can't make a turtle come out,
You can't make a turtle come out,
You can coax him or call him
or shake him or shout,
But you can't make a turtle come out,
come out,
You can't make a turtle come out.

By the way, what may a turtle say
when it comes out?

Listen to Predict

Look at the pictures.

Listen.

Say what will happen next.

Using **We** and **They**

Use the words **we** and **they** when you talk about more than one.

We talk.
They meow.

Write **we** or **they** for the underlined words.

1. <u>Pat and I</u> walk home together.

_____ walk home together.

2. <u>Joe and Ben</u> ride their bikes home.

_____ ride their bikes home.

3. Some days <u>Pat and I</u> see Joe and Ben.

Some days _____ see Joe and Ben.

4. Then <u>our friends</u> smile at us.

Then _____ smile at us.

Listening to Animal Jokes

Look at the pictures.

Listen.

Do you know the answers?

1. What game do the cows like to play most?

moo-sical chairs

2. Where does the sheep go to get its hair cut?

to the baa-baa shop

3. What did the teacher say about the kitten's test?

purr-fect

Poetry Place

Giraffes Don't Huff

by Karla Kuskin

Giraffes don't huff or hoot or howl
They never grump, they never growl
They never roar, they never riot.
They eat green leaves
And just keep quiet.

Words That Sound Alike

Some words sound alike, but they have different spellings and meanings.

The words **see** and **sea** sound alike.
I see lots of fish in the sea.

Look at the pictures.
Write the correct word to finish the sentence.

1. Who _____ the cake?

     eight   ate

2. The _____ runs fast.

     deer   dear

3. Did you _____ my friend?

     meat   meet

Name _____

What Have I Learned?

Write an action word in each sentence.

cleans	sits	eats	runs
clean	sit	eat	run

1. They _____ .

2. The duck _____ .

3. We _____ .

4. The cats _____ .

CHAPTER 7

Personal Note

Listen to Write

There's an Alligator Under My Bed

by Mercer Mayer

1.

2.

3.

4.

5.

The Story and You

Imagine that something scary
is hiding under the bed.
What is it?
Draw a picture.
Write about your picture.

Name _____

Look and Learn

The boy wrote a note to his mom, too.
Read what it says.

Dear Mom,
    Look out! There is a big alligator in the garage. Do not go in. I already told Dad.
                                Love,
                                Your son

Prewriting

People write notes for different reasons.

Plan a note you will write.

Dear Bob,
Thank you for the pet fish.
Your friend,
Pete

Mark,
Meet me at the pool.
Your friend,
Ira

Dear Mom,
I went to the park.
Nina

**Make an X to show why
you want to write your note.**

☐ To send a special message

☐ To share something you know

☐ To ask for a favor

☐ To say thank you

Now write the name of the person who will get your note.

_____

- -

_____

Name _____

Writing

Look back at page 104. Think about why you want to write a note and who will get the note. Now write your note.

Dear _____,

Your friend,

Describing Words

A **describing word** tells something about a naming word.

The word **fresh** tells more about the naming word **fruit**.

The alligator likes **fresh** fruit.

Circle the describing words.

1. Alligators have bright eyes.

2. They have sharp claws.

3. They all have cold skin.

4. This alligator has a silly grin.

Name _____

More Describing Words

A **describing word** tells something about a naming word.

Look at the picture.
Write a describing word
to finish each sentence.

pretty	nice
happy	sad

1. The boy draws a _____ face.

2. The alligator looks _____ .

3. He wants to make a _____ picture.

4. The _____ boy helps him draw.

Action Words with More Than One

Write an action word from the box
to finish each sentence.

swings	runs	sleeps	sings
swing	run	sleep	sing

1. The birds _____.

2. The children _____.

3. The squirrels _____.

4. The rabbits _____.

Name _____

Talking About Colors

Color words are one kind of describing words.

Color the picture.
Use these colors.

Use color words to talk about your picture.

Talking About Sizes and Shapes

Size and shape **words can be describing words, too.**

Look at the words in the box.

big	round	long
little	square	tall

Use size and shape words to talk about the picture.

Name _____

Listening to Visualize

Listen. Close your eyes.
Try to see what the poem tells about.

Blowing Bubbles

by Margaret Hillert

Dip your pipe and gently blow.
Watch the tiny bubble grow
Big and bigger, round and fat,
Rainbow-colored, and then—
SPLAT!

Draw a picture to show what the poem tells about.

Talk about your picture.
Use color words and size and shape words.

Listening for Sensory Words

Listen.

Draw a line from one little picture to one list.

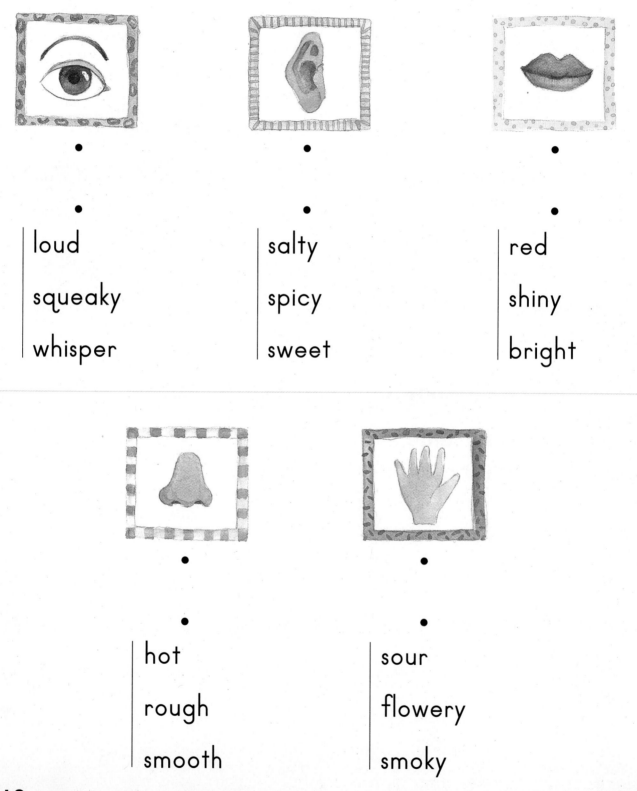

loud

squeaky

whisper

salty

spicy

sweet

red

shiny

bright

hot

rough

smooth

sour

flowery

smoky

Poetry Place

The Alligator

by Mary Macdonald

The alligator chased his tail

Which hit him on the snout;

He nibbled, gobbled, swallowed it,

And turned right inside-out.

Opposites

Some words have **opposite** meanings.

The words **neat** and **messy** have opposite meanings.

The boy has a **neat** room.
The boy has a **messy** room.

Find the word with the line under it.
Circle the word that means the opposite.

1. Look at the big alligator.   little   green

2. She has a long tail.   tall   short

3. See her happy face.   sad   sleepy

4. She is eating a cold treat.   hot   new

What Have I Learned?

Write a describing word
to finish each sentence.

Describing Words

warm	nice
dark	red
good	

Dear friend,
Here are some
describing words
to use.
Love,
The Alligator
Under the Bed

1. I do not like the _____ garage.

2. I like the girl's _____ room.

3. She gives me _____ treats.

4. She gives me _____ apples.

5. I want a _____ friend.

Friendly Letter

Listen to Write

We Are Best Friends

by Aliki

1.

2.

3.

4.

DEAR ROBERT,
I HOPE YOU STILL REMEMBER ME.
I LIKE MY NEW HOUSE NOW.
I LIKE MY NEW SCHOOL NOW.
AT FIRST I DIDN'T LIKE ANYTHING.
BUT NOW I HAVE A FRIEND, ALEX.
YOU ARE MY BEST FRIEND,
BUT ALEX IS NICE.

IT IS FUN TO HAVE SOMEONE
TO PLAY WITH AGAIN.
IT'S NOT SO LONELY.
LOVE, PETER

The Story and You

Which would you do if your best friend moved away?

Circle one or more pictures.

Write to tell about how you would feel.

_____

- -

_____

- -

_____

- -

_____

- -

_____

- -

_____

Look and Learn

Will missed his friends back at his old school.
Here is a letter he wrote to one friend.

September 19, 1999

Dear Nick,

    I miss you. My new house is nice. I have my own room. I met a boy at school. Robert and I are going on a bike ride Saturday. Write back.

       Your best friend,
Will

Prewriting

Look at and talk about the parts of a letter.

_____

(Date)

(Greeting) **Dear** _____ ,

(Body, or what you want to say)

_____

_____

(Closing,)

(Your Name)

Who will get a letter from you?

Write the name in the space.

Think about what you want to say.

Name _____

Writing

What have you been doing?
Your friend might like to know.
Write a letter to your friend.

Dear _____ ,

Your friend,

Adjectives to Compare

Describing words are **adjectives**.
Adjectives that end with **-er** compare two things.

Use **bigger** to compare two frogs.
   This is a big frog.
   That frog is bigger.

Write each adjective on this page and on the next page.
Add **-er** to compare the two things.

1.

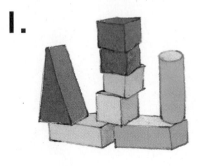

_____

_ _ _ _ _ _ _ _ _ _ _ _ _ _

tall   _____

Name _____

2.

fast

_____

3.

slow

_____

4.

deep

_____

Adjectives to Compare

Adjectives that end with -est compare more than two.

Use highest to compare the jumps of three frogs.

A frog jumps high.
The next frog jumps higher.
The last frog jumps highest.

Write each adjective on this page and on the next page.

Add -est to compare three things.

1.

small   smaller   _____

2.

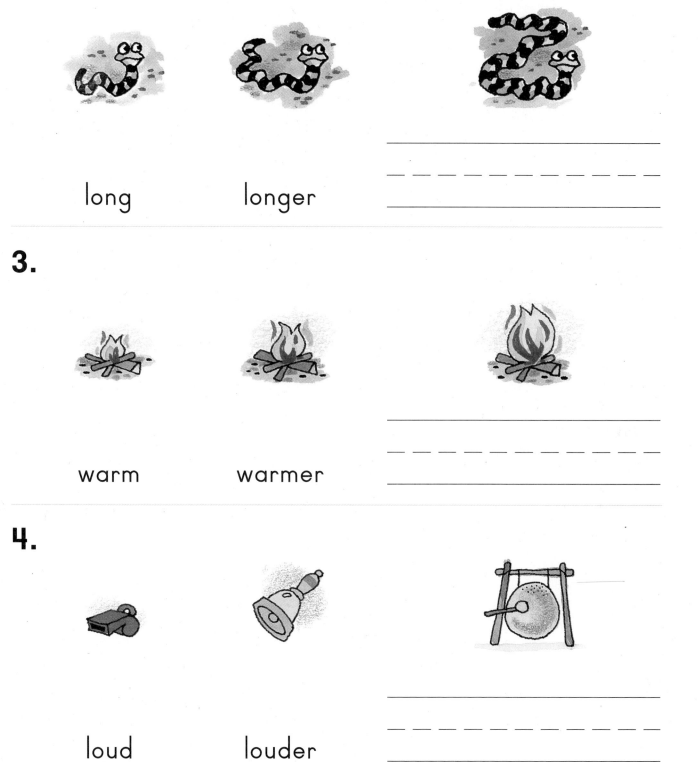

long   longer

3.

warm   warmer

4.

loud   louder

Identifying Adjectives

Draw a line under the adjective,
or describing word, in each sentence.
Write another adjective for the sentence.

1. I wear my blue shirt.

_____

2. My friend has on short pants.

_____

3. I draw a happy face.

_____

4. My friend draws a silly cat.

_____

5. We are best friends.

_____

Name _____

Hearing and Making Introductions

Listen.
Draw a line to match the words to the correct picture.

1. Hi. My name is Robert.

This is my frog, Greenie.

•   •

2. Hello. I am Dr. Perez.

This is my helper, Mrs. White.

•   •

3. Greenie, this is Hopper.

You can be friends.

•   •

Now you try.
Write in names.

Hello. My name is _____.

This is my friend _____.

Listening to Rhymes About Weather

Listen and say each rhyme.
Draw a picture to go with the rhyme you like best.

1. It's raining, it's pouring,
The old man is snoring.

2. March winds and April showers
Bring forth May flowers.

3. The north wind doth blow,
And we shall have snow.

Poetry Place

Together

by Paul Engle

Because we do
All things together
All things improve,
Even weather.

Our daily meat
And bread taste better,
Trees are greener,
Rain is wetter.

Contractions with Not

A **contraction** is a way to make one word out of two words.

The word **isn't** is another way of saying **is not**.

It is not raining.
It isn't raining.

Draw a line under the contraction in each sentence.
Write what two words the contraction stands for.

1. Robert doesn't feel happy. _____

2. Peter isn't going to stay. _____

3. The friends don't smile. _____

4. Peter doesn't want to go. _____

What Have I Learned?

Use **-er** to compare two.
Use **-est** to compare more than two.

Write the correct adjective.

1. Robert's frog is _____ than Amy's.

       smaller   smallest

2. Amy finds the _____ frog in the garden.

       bigger   biggest

3. Big frogs make the _____ jumps.

       longer   longest

4. Big frogs croak _____ than little ones.

       louder   loudest

Report

Listen to Write

Never Kiss an Alligator!

by Colleen Stanley Bare

I.

Alligators

Alligator

2.

Crocodile

3.

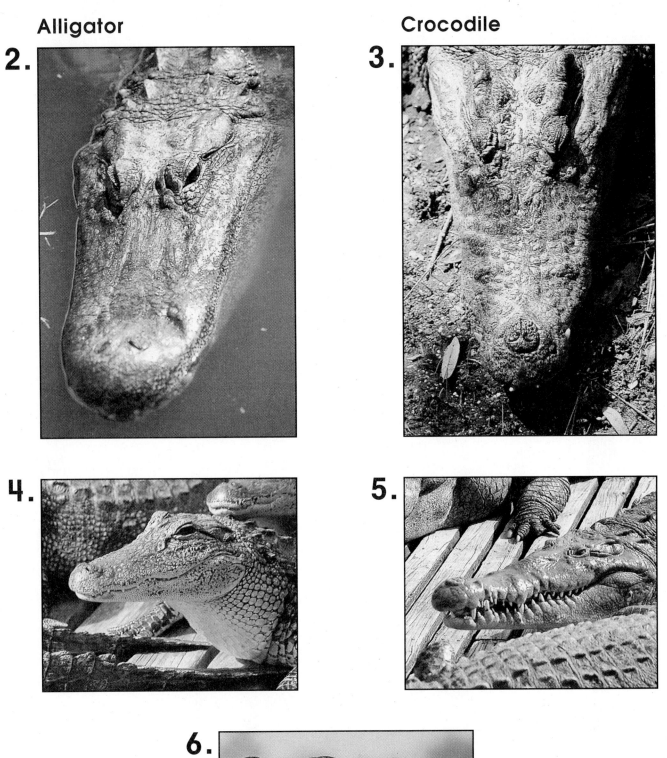

4.

5.

6.

Baby alligator

The Story and You

What is the most interesting thing you found out about alligators?
Draw a picture.
Write to tell about the picture.

Name _____

Look and Learn

Could you write a report about alligators?
Here is what one first grader wrote.

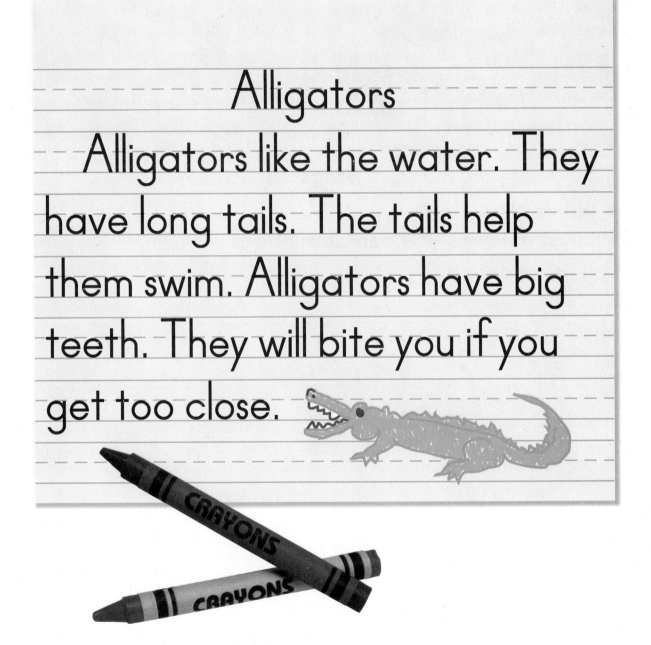

Alligators

Alligators like the water. They have long tails. The tails help them swim. Alligators have big teeth. They will bite you if you get too close.

Prewriting

Frogs

Look at the picture.

Find out as much as you can about frogs.

Write a list of details.

Writing

Write a report about frogs.

Use the details on page 136 to help you.

Frogs

Parts of a Sentence: Naming Part

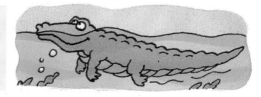

The **naming part** of a sentence tells who or what is doing the action.

The alligator is the naming part of the sentence.

The alligator swims fast.

Draw a line under the naming part of each sentence.

1. A mother watches her eggs.

2. One egg hatches.

3. A baby comes out.

4. The little alligator can bite.

5. The grass hides the baby.

Parts of a Sentence: Action Part

The **action part** of a sentence tells what the naming part does.

| The action part of the sentence is **runs on land.**

The alligator runs on land.

Draw a line under the action part of each sentence.

1. Some alligators live in zoos.

2. People watch the alligators.

3. Alligators grow very big.

4. Children look for the biggest one.

5. One girl takes a picture.

Adjectives to Compare

Use **-er** to compare two.

Use **-est** to compare more than two.

Write the correct adjective.

1. Alligators are _____ than crocodiles.

slower   slowest

2. The alligators can swim _____ than you.

faster   fastest

3. This alligator has the _____ tail of all.

longer   longest

Giving an Oral Report

Here are two groups of pictures.
Choose one group.
Look carefully to find out about the animal.

Tigers

Elephants

**Write notes about the animal
you chose. Then use your notes
to give a report about the animal.**

Name

Changing Sentences

Listen.

Change each asking sentence into a telling sentence.

1. Can all alligators swim?

2. Do crocodiles have big teeth?

3. Do people study alligators?

Listen.

Change each telling sentence into an asking sentence.

1. Alligators will bite.

2. Some alligators live in the zoo.

Poetry Place

Ten Little Gators

One little, two little,
three little gators,

Four little, five little,
six little gators,

Seven little, eight little,
nine little gators,

Ten little gators' grins.

Different Meaning

Some words can mean more than one thing.

Draw a line to match each sentence to the correct picture.

1. Can alligators play on <u>swings</u>?　•　　•

The alligator <u>swings</u> its tail.　•　　•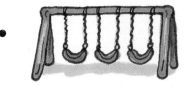

2. A toy <u>top</u> spins.　•　　　　•

Just the <u>top</u> of the head shows.　•　•

3. I'll <u>watch</u> the alligator.　•　　•

My <u>watch</u> is new.　•　　　　•

Name _____

What Have I Learned?

A sentence has a naming part and an action part.

Look at the words with a line under them.
Write **N** if they are the naming part.
Write **A** if they are the action part.

1. [   ] <u>Many animals</u> live in the zoo.

2. [   ] The reptiles <u>live in one part</u>.

3. [   ] <u>Zookeepers</u> take care of them.

4. [   ] Children <u>come to look and learn</u>.

5. [   ] Visitors <u>take pictures</u>.

Story Ending

Listen to Write

The Chick and the Duckling

by Mirra Ginsburg

1.

2.

3.

4.

The Story and You

The Chick and the Duckling like to do things together.
Draw and write about something you like to do with friends.

_____

- -

_____

_____

- -

_____

_____

Name _____

Look and Learn

Here is a story of the Chick and the Duckling.
Make up a new ending.
In the box, write or draw the new ending.

The Chick and the Duckling

Beginning	The Duckling comes out. The Chick comes out.
Middle	They walk. They dig. They catch butterflies.

Ending

Listen to Practice

Look and listen.

What is the main idea?

Mark it with an X.

1.

☐ The Duckling came out first.

☐ The little birds do things together.

☐ The Chick digs for worms.

2.

☐ Little birds eat and sleep.

☐ The mother bird can fly.

☐ The mother takes care of her babies.

Listen to Practice

Listen.

Write 1, 2, and 3 to show the correct order.

Prewriting

Look at the pictures.

Read the beginning and middle of the story.

How will the story end? Write some ideas.

The Walk

Beginning

The ducks walk.

Middle

The chick walks, too.
The ducks and the chick
are by the water.

Ending

_____

_ _ _ _ _ _ _ _ _ _ _ _ _ _ _ _ _ _ _

_____

_ _ _ _ _ _ _ _ _ _ _ _ _ _ _ _ _ _ _

_____

Writing

How does the story on page 154 end?
Draw a picture and write your ending.

Action Words

Another name for an action word is **verb**.

A verb in the present tells what a person, animal, or thing does.

The chick walks.

Read the sentences. Write the verbs.

_____

1. The chicks play all day.

_____

2. She likes games.

_____

3. Then the chicks rest.

_____

4. Mother calls them for dinner.

Name _____

Verbs

Verbs in the past end in -ed.

▌ **A verb in the past tells what a person, animal, or thing did.**

The ducks walked.

Read each sentence. Add -ed to the verb.

1. Last night the little ducks _____.

quack

2. They _____ their mother.

need

3. Mother Duck _____ them.

help

4. She _____ off the light.

turn

Parts of a Sentence

Make sentences to tell about the picture.

Draw a line to match a naming part with an action part.

Naming Part		**Action Part**
A dog	•	• eats lunch.
The farmer	•	• swim in a pond.
Two ducks	•	• barks.

Write the three sentences.

1. _____

2. _____

3. _____

Name _____

Using See and Saw

The verb **see** tells us what is happening now, or in the present.

▌ I see the butterfly.

The verb **saw** tells what happened in the past.

▌ Last month I saw a caterpillar.

Write see or saw to complete each sentence.

1. Once I _____ a nest full of eggs.

2. Now I _____ some chicks.

3. I _____ red leaves on the tree now.

4. Last week I _____ green leaves.

Using Go and Went

The verb **go** tells about the present.

▌ Today we go to the farm.

The verb **went** tells about the past.

▌ Last year we went to the zoo.

Circle the verb in each sentence.
Write **present** or **past** to tell about each word.

1. I often go to the ocean.

2. Last year I went on a plane.

3. My brother went camping.

4. I go to the woods to camp.

5. We go camping every summer.

Name _____

Using **Is** and **Are** and **Was** and **Were**

The verbs is and are tell about the present.
Is tells about one. Are tells about more than one.

| A chick **is** in the yard.
The ducks **are** in the pond.

The verbs was and were tell about the past.
Was tells about one. Were tells about more than one.

| The hen **was** on a nest.
Some eggs **were** in the nest.

Circle the verb in each sentence.
Write **present** or **past** to tell about each word.

1. The sun is hot today. _____

2. The ducks are in the water. _____

3. Last winter was very cold. _____

Storytelling

Here are some tips to help you be a good storyteller.

1. Listen to or read the story again.

2. Think about the order in which things happen.

3. Speak the way you think those in the story would sound.

4. Move your hands and arms to help show what happens.

5. Use your face to show how the characters feel.

6. Use a loud or soft voice to get listeners excited.

Think about the story **The Chick and the Duckling.**
Retell the story in your own words.

Ducks in the Rain

by James S. Tippett

Ducks are dabbling in the rain,
Dibbling, dabbling in the rain.
Drops of water from each back
Scatter as ducks flap and quack.

I can only stand and look
From my window at the brook,
For I cannot flap and quack
And scatter raindrops from my back.

Irregular Verbs

Circle the correct verb for each sentence.

1. A sad chick _____, "No more rain!"

     say   said

2. At last the sun _____ out.

     come   came

3. The duck _____ to meet the chick.

     swim   swam

4. Now the duck and chick look and _____.

     dig   dug

5. They _____ some worms and eat.

     find   found

Name _____

What Have I Learned?

Read the story.
Draw a line under each verb.
Does the verb tell about the present or the past?
Write each verb in the correct box.

1. The chick and the duck work in the yard.

2. Last week, the chick planted seeds.

3. The duck watered the seeds.

4. Now they wait for pretty flowers.

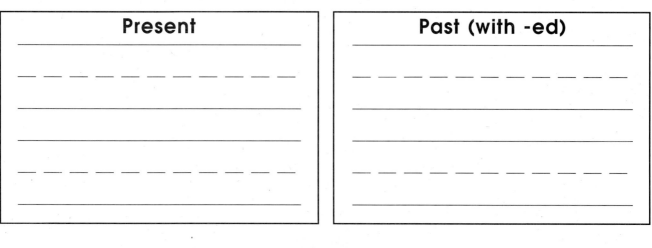

Present	Past (with -ed)

Book Report

Listen to Write

Who Took the Farmer's Hat?

by Joan L. Nôdset

illustrated by Fritz Siebel

1.

The Story and You

If you found the farmer's hat, what would you use it for?
Draw and write what you would do with the hat.

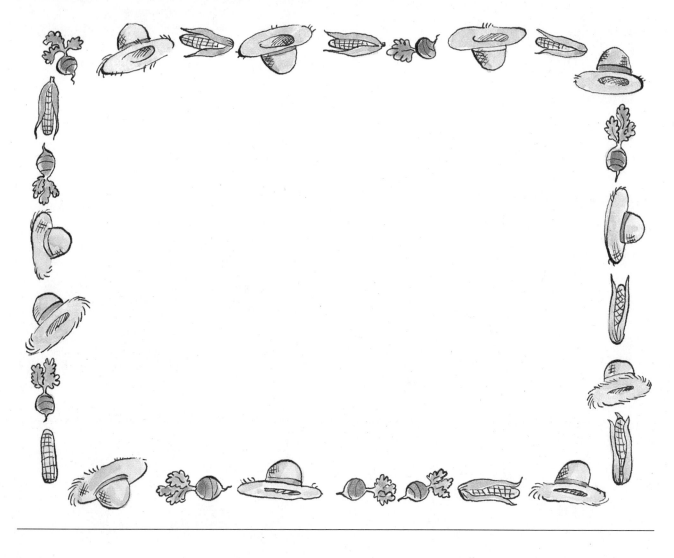

_____

- -

_____

- -

_____

- -

_____

Name _____

Look and Learn

One way to let friends know about a book is to write a book report. Here is a book report about the story you heard. The name of the book is underlined.

The title of my book is <u>Who Took the Farmer's Hat?</u> It is by Joan L. Nodset. The story is about a farmer and his lost hat. Some animals see the hat. They do not know it is really a hat. The farmer finds his hat in a tree. The birds make it into a nest. It has eggs in it.

    I like this book. It has funny parts. It has good pictures.

Prewriting

Make notes about a book that you have read.
The notes will help you write your own book report.

Title _____

Author _____

Who is in the story? _____

Where does the story take place?

_____

What is the problem? _____

How does the story end?

_____

Name _____

Writing

Write your book report.
Use your notes on page 170.
Underline the name of the book.

The title of my book is

It is by

The story is about

Pronouns

A **pronoun** takes the place of a noun, or a naming word.

He, she, and **it** are pronouns.
Farmer Bill lost a hat.
He lost a hat.

Write the pronoun to take the place of the underlined words.

1. The <u>wind</u> grabs the hat.

_____

_ _ _ _ _ _

_____

2. The <u>farmer</u> runs.

_____

_ _ _ _ _ _

_____

3. <u>Mrs. Mouse</u> did not see the hat.

_____

_ _ _ _ _ _

_____

4. The <u>hat</u> is in a tree.

_____

_ _ _ _ _ _

_____

Name _____

Pronouns

Remember, pronouns take the place of nouns.

The words **I** and **you** are pronouns.
So are the words **we** and **they.**

"**I** lost my hat," said the farmer.
"**We** can help look for the hat,"
said the animals.

Write **I, you, we,** or **they** in the sentences.

1. "_____ want my hat," said the farmer.

2. "_____ did not see it," said the animals.

3. "_____ can help me," said the farmer.

4. _____ all helped the farmer look.

© Loyola Press

Verbs

Write the correct verb for each sentence.

1. The dog watched as the farmer _____.

       works   worked

2. The wind blew and _____ the hat.

       lifts   lifted

3. The hat flipped and _____ in a field.

       lands   landed

4. Now a mouse _____ in the hat.

       lives   lived

5. The farmer _____ the new hat he has now.

       likes   liked

Talking About the Library

What different things can people do in a library?

Talk with a partner.

Then share your ideas with the class.

Tell what you like to do in the library.

Talking About Parts of a Book

Talk about this book cover.
What does it tell you?

Look at this page.
It tells the parts of the book.
On which page does each different part begin?

Name _____

Discussing a Picture Walk

One way to find out about a book
is first to look at the pictures.

Work with a partner.
Find a book you have not read.
Look at the cover and the pictures inside.
Talk about these things.

- What might the book be about?

- Who might be the characters?

- Where do you think the action takes place?

- Is the book about real things or make-believe things?

- Might it make you laugh or help you learn?

- Do you want to read the book? Tell why.

Distinguishing Between Fiction and Nonfiction Titles

Some books tell stories.
Other books give facts.

Listen to each book title.

Do you think the book tells a story or gives facts?

What makes you think so?

Pinkie the Pig Goes to School

Happy Birthday, Charlie Chick

How to Milk a Cow

What Do Farmers Do?

All Kinds of Weather

Who Took the Farmer's Hat?

Name _____

Poetry Place

Wouldn't You

by John Ciardi

If I

Could go

As high

And low

As the wind

As the wind

As the wind

Can blow—

I'd go!

a b c d e f g h i j k l m n o p q r s t u v w x y z

ABC Word Order

Write these letters in abc order.

d   b   g   e

_____

_____

Look at the first letter of each word.
Now write each group of words in abc order.

| hat |
| farmer |
| boat |

| wind |
| round |
| sky |

_____   _____

_____   _____

_____   _____

Name _____

What Have I Learned?

Write the pronoun that takes the place
of the underlined word or words.

| He | She |
| They | It |

1. The <u>wind</u> blew off the hat.

_____

2. The <u>farmer</u> said, "Oh, No!"

_____

3. The <u>cat and dog</u> ran.

_____

4. <u>Mrs. Bird</u> said, "I have the hat."

_____

Write the correct pronoun.

1. "_____ have no hat," said the farmer.

            I   We

2. "_____ need a new hat, farmer," said the man.

    They   You

Grammar Handbook

Contents

Sentences

A **sentence** is a group of words that tells a whole idea. A sentence begins with a capital letter and ends with an end mark. There are four kinds of sentences.

A **telling sentence** tells something. A telling sentence ends with [.].

Last night I took a trip to Mars.

An **asking sentence** asks a question. An asking sentence ends with [?].

What did you say?

A sentence may show strong feelings. A sentence that shows strong feelings ends with $\boxed{!}$.

What an amazing trip!

A sentence may tell someone to do something. A sentence that tells someone to do something ends with $\boxed{.}$.

Tell me about Mars.

A sentence has two parts. The **naming part** tells who or what does the action. The **action part** tells what the naming part does.

My teddy bear and I dream of Mars.

The naming part of this sentence, **My teddy bear and I**, tells who does the action. The action part, **dream of Mars**, tells what they do.

Nouns

A **noun** is a naming word.
Nouns name people, places, animals,
and things.

> The boy wanted a pet.

The word **boy** names a person.
Pet names an animal.

> He bought a dog and a leash
> at Best Pets.

The word **leash** names a thing.
Best Pets names a place.

Add **-s** to most nouns to name
more than one.

> dog   dogs

A proper noun names a special person
place, animal, or thing. A proper noun
begins with a capital letter.

> My dog gave his toy to Marie.

The names of the days of the week and
months of the year are proper nouns.
Titles of people are proper nouns.

Pronouns

A **pronoun** is a word
that takes the place of a noun.

Give the camera to Dan.
Give it to Dan.

The word **it** is a pronoun.
It takes the place of **camera.**

Here are some other pronouns.

I   me   you   he   she   we   they

- **You** can name one or more than one.
- Write **I** with a capital letter.
- Always name yourself last.

Verbs

A **verb** tells what a person, animal,
or thing does.

I mix the paint and clean the brushes.

The words **mix** and **clean** tell what I do.
Mix and **clean** are verbs.

Some verbs do not show action.

The brushes are on the table.

The verb **are** does not show action.

Many verbs that tell what one person, animal, or thing does end with -s.

Dory paints beautiful pictures.

Many verbs that tell what more than one person, animal, or thing do now do not end with -s.

Dory and I paint together.

Many verbs that tell what people, animals, and things did in the past end with -ed.

Dory painted a picture of my sister.

Some verbs in the past do not end with -ed.

went   saw   was   were

Adjectives

An **adjective** is a describing word.
An adjective tells about a noun.

Two little boys play in the snow.

The adjectives **two** and **little** tell
about the noun **boys**.

Adjectives can tell the color, size,
or shape of someone or something.
Adjectives can tell how many people
or things there are. Some adjectives
describe the weather or what our
senses tell us.

Adjectives that end with **-er** compare
two people, places, animals, or things.

What does the younger boy do?

Adjectives that end with **-est** compare
more than two.

He wants to build the highest wall of all.

Index

Acknowledgments

16 "Little Chickens." Author unknown.

18 From *Albert's Field Trip*, by Leslie Tryon. Copyright © 1993, by Leslie Tryon. Reprinted with permission of Atheneum Books for Young Readers, Simon & Schuster Children's Publishing Division.

27 "The Wheels on the Bus." Traditional song adaptation. Author unknown.

31 "One, Two, Three, Four." Author unknown.

34 From *Happy Birthday, Jesse Bear*, text by Nancy White Carlstrom and illustrations by Bruce Degen. Text copyright © 1994, by Nancy White Carlstrom; Illustrations copyright © 1994, by Bruce Degen. Reprinted with permission of Simon & Schuster Books for Young Readers, Simon & Schuster Children's Publishing Division.

43 "Every Week Song" by Myra Cohn Livingston.

47 "The Wish" by Ann Friday. Public Domain.

50 From *My Brown Bear Barney* by Dorothy Butler. Illustrated by Elizabeth Fuller. Text copyright © 1988 by Dorothy Butler; Illustrations copyright © 1988 by Elizabeth Fuller. Reprinted with permission of Greenwillow Books, a division of William Morrow & Company, Inc.

65 "My Teddy Bear" from *Rhymes About Us* by Marchette Chute. Published 1974 by E.P. Dutton. Copyright © 1974 by Marchette Chute. Reprinted by permission of Elizabeth Roach.

68 From *Too Many Tamales* by Gary Soto. Illustrated by Ed Martinez. Copyright © 1993. Used by permission of Penguin Putnam Inc.

78 "Clap Your Hands." Copyright, 1948 Ruth Crawford Seeger. From *American Folk Songs for Children*, by Ruth Crawford Seeger, Doubleday.

81 "Mix a Pancake." Reprinted with the permission of Simon & Schuster Books for Young Readers, an Imprint of Simon & Schuster Children's Publishing Division from *Sing-Song* by Christina G. Rossetti (New York, Macmillan 1924).

84 "I Speak, I Say, I Talk" by Arnold Shapiro. From *Once Upon A Time*, Volume 1 of *Childcraft—The How and Why Library* © 1996 World Book, Inc. By permission of the publisher.

97 "Giraffes Don't Huff" from *Roar and More* by Karla Kuskin. Copyright © 1956, 1990 by Karla Kuskin. Used by permission of HarperCollins Publishers.

100 From *There's An Alligator Under My Bed* by Mercer Mayer. Copyright © 1987 by Mercer Mayer. Used by permission of Dial Books for Young Readers, a division of Penguin Books USA Inc.

111 "Blowing Bubbles" by Margaret Hillert. Used by permission of the author who controls all rights.

113 "The Alligator" by Mary Macdonald.

116 From *We Are Best Friends* by Aliki. Copyright © 1982 by Aliki Brandenberg. Reprinted by permission of Greenwillow Books, a division of William Morrow & Company Inc.

129 "Together" from *Embrace* by Paul Engle. Copyright © 1969 by Paul Engle. Reprinted by permission of Random House, Inc.

132 From *Never Kiss An Alligator* by Colleen Stanley Bare. Copyright © 1989 by Colleen Stanley Bare. Used by permission of Cobblehill Books, an affiliate of Dutton Children's Books, a division of Penguin USA Inc.

145 "Ten Little Gators." Traditional Rhyme.

148 From *The Chick and the Duckling*, text by Mirra Ginsburg and illustrated by Jose Aruego and Ariane Dewey. Text and illustrations copyright © 1972, as appears in Licensor's edition of the Work. Reprinted with permission of Simon & Schuster Books for Young Readers, Simon & Schuster Children's Publishing Division.

163 "Ducks in the Rain" from *Crickety Cricket! The Best-Loved Poems of James S. Tippett.* Copyright 1933, copyright renewed © 1973 by Martha K. Tippett. Used by permission of HarperCollins Publishers.

166 From *Who Took the Farmer's Hat?* by Joan Nödset and illustrations by Fritz Siebel. Text copyright © 1963 by Joan M. Lexau. Illustrations copyright © 1963 by Fritz Siebel. Used by permission of HarperCollins Publishers.

179 "Wouldn't You?" from *You Read To Me, I'll Read To You* by John Ciardi. Copyright © 1962 by John Ciardi. Used by permission of HarperCollins Publishers.

All attempts possible have been made to contact author and publisher for cited works in this book.

Art & Photography

Cover: Jessie Coates, *Old Port Hudson*. Private collection/J. Coates/SuperStock.

Photographs: i image provided by MetaTools. ii image © 1998 PhotoDisc, Inc. iii image provided by MetaTools. v image © 1998 PhotoDisc, Inc. vi image provided by MetaTools. ix image © 1998 PhotoDisc, Inc. xi image © 1998 PhotoDisc, Inc. 9 image provided by MetaTools. 26 image © 1998 PhotoDisc, Inc. 29 (T, B) Corel Corporation, (M) image provided by MetaTools. 36 (TL, TR; BR) image © 1998 PhotoDisc, Inc., (BL) image provided by MetaTools. 47 Allan Landau Photography. 48 image provided by MetaTools. 76 All images © 1998 PhotoDisc, Inc. 79 All images© 1998 PhotoDisc, Inc. 86 Image provided by Image Club Graphics, a division of Adobe Systems, Inc. 88 (TL, M, R) Corel Corporation, (BL) image provided by MetaTools, (BM, R) Corel Corporation 92 image © 1998 PhotoDisc, Inc. 93 image provided by MetaTools 111 (frame) image provided by MetaTools, (boy) image © Cleo Photography/PhotoEdit 121 image © 1998 PhotoDisc, Inc. 128 image © 1998 PhotoDisc, Inc. 134 image © Chris Johns/Tony Stone Images 135 image provided by MetaTools 141(TL) image © Mervyn Rees/Tony Stone Images (TM) image © SuperStock, Inc (TR) image © John Warden/SuperStock, Inc. (BL) image © Alan Briere/ SuperStock, Inc. (BM) image © Anne B. Keiser/ SuperStock, Inc. (BR) image © Mark Newman/ SuperStock, Inc. 142 images © 1998 PhotoDisc, Inc. 143 (L) image © Alan Briere/ SuperStock, Inc., (M) image © 1998 PhotoDisc, Inc., (R) image © 1998 PhotoDisc, Inc., (frames) images provided by Metatools 155 Allan Landau Photography 161 images © 1998 PhotoDisc, Inc. 165 image © 1998 PhotoDisc, Inc. 176 image © 1998 PhotoDisc, Inc. 177 image © 1998 PhotoDisc, Inc. 180 Allan Landau Photography 183 image provided by MetaTools.

Illustrations: Elizabeth Allen, i(M, B) viii, 10, 16, 118, 122-123, 127, 179. **Ellen Appleby,** iii, 40, 46. **Lois Axeman,** 12, 17, 37, 44, 72, 140, 147. **Susan Banta,** ii(T), 8, 11, 20, 26, 32, 39, 129. **Shirley Beckes,** 7, 13, 42, 49, 86, 92, 102, 109, 158. **Nan Brooks,** 38, 45. **Priscilla Burris,** 113, 146, 163. **Susan Calitri,** 153(B), 154, 159, 162, 165. **Olivia Cole,** viii(T), 14, 15, 23, 28, 64, 124-125. **Julie Durell,** v, 71, 75, 81, 168, 178(B). **Patrick Girouard,** ii(M), 22, 27, 33, 70, 74, 77, 80, 106, 134, 138, 153(T), 172, 175. **Melanie Hall,** vi, 84-85, 89, 173, 177, 181. **Megan Halsey,** iv(M), 59, 63. **Paul Harvey,** 174, 178(T). **Ruth Linstromberg,** 90, 95. **Steven Mach,** 87, 94, 97, 98, 126, 131. **Robert Masheris,** 182, 184, 185, 186, 187. **Anni Matsick,** 25, 31, 41, 56, 62, 83. **Judith Moffitt,** 110, 144, 151, 157. **Keiko Motoyama,** x(T), 91, 99, 112, 150, 156, 164. **Sherry Niedigh,** 24, 30, 36, 43. **Diane Palmisciano,** iv(B), 54, 60, 65, 73, 78, 82. **Diana Philbrook,** 55, 61, 66. **Cary Pillo,** ix, 108, 139. **Margaret Sanfilippo,** iv(T), 52, 58, 65, 130. **Katherine Tillotson,** vii(T), x(M), 114, 145, 152. **Jackie Urbanovic,** vii(B), 96, 107, 136, 160.